# ▷ Contents

Any words appearing in the text in bold, **like this**, are explained in the Glossary.

# Fast bikes

There are many different types of motorcycles. Each type is designed for a different style of riding. Touring motorcycles are designed for comfort on long journeys, off-roaders are designed for fun on dirt tracks, and cruisers are designed for low-speed riding with ease.

However, in sports motorcycle design, **performance** comes first. Sports motorcycles **accelerate** fast and hug the curves of road and racetrack. Their size, weight, power, and shape are carefully designed to make them a thrilling ride. These high-performance motorcycles are often called "Superbikes". This is also the name of a type of motorcycle racing (see page 9) that is based on **production motorcycles**. Today, most of the world's motorcycles come from Japan and Italy. They are built by manufacturers such as Honda, Yamaha, Suzuki, and Kawasaki in Japan, and Ducati, MV Agusta, Benelli, and Cagiva in Italy.

## Fireblade ▽

When the Honda CBR900RR Fireblade was introduced in 1992, it started a revolution in sports motorcycle design. The Fireblade was lighter than older motorcycles, so it did not have to be as powerful. It was the first of a new generation of sports motorcycles whose lightness resulted in a more agile sports performance. The Fireblade has been updated year after year.

The first Fireblade had an 893**cc** engine. By 2007, it had been updated to a bigger 998cc powerplant. The letters "cc" mean "cubic centimetres". The number of ccs shows how big the engine is.

# Designed For Success

# Sup~~erbik~~es

**Heinemann**
LIBRARY

## Ian Graham

**www.heinemann.co.uk/library**
Visit our website to find out more information about **Heinemann Library** books.

To order:
 Phone 44 (0) 1865 888066
 Send a fax to 44 (0) 1865 314091
Visit the Heinemann Bookshop at www.heinemann.co.uk/library to browse our catalogue
and order online.

First published in Great Britain by Heinemann Library, Halley Court,
Jordan Hill, Oxford, OX2 8EJ, part of Harcourt Education.
Heinemann is a registered trademark of Harcourt
Education Ltd.

© Harcourt Education Ltd 2008
The moral right of the proprietor has been asserted.

Editorial: Andrew Farrow and Dan Nunn
Design: Steven Mead and Geoff Ward
Illustrations: Geoff Ward
Picture Research: Melissa Allison
Production: Alison Parsons

Originated by Modern Age
Printed and bound in China by South China
    Printing Company

ISBN 978 0 431 16583 7 (hardback)
13 12 11 10 09 08
10 9 8 7 6 5 4 3 2 1

ISBN 978 0 431 16591 2 (paperback)
13 12 11 10 09 08
10 9 8 7 6 5 4 3 2 1

**British Library Cataloguing-in-Publication Data**
Graham, Ian, 1953 –
    Superbikes. – (Designed for success) 2nd edition
    1. Superbikes – Juvenile literature
    I. Title
    629.2'275
A full catalogue record for this book is available from the
British Library.

**Acknowledgements**
The publishers would like to thank the following for permission to
reproduce photographs:
© Alvey & Towers pp. **1**, **3**, **11** (top), **13** (bottom), **14** (top); © Auto
Express pp. **15** (top), **15** (bottom), **18**; © BMW AG p. **17** (bottom); ©
Corbis pp. **8**, **25** (top), **26**, **27** (top), **28**, **29**; © Corbis/Bettman p. **29**;
© D&W Images/James Weishaar p. **27** (bottom); © Daimler Chrysler
p. **17** (top); © Ducati p. **5** (bottom); © EMAP p. **6**; © EMAP/MDE pp.
**10**, **14** (bottom); © EPA p. **22**; © Eye Ubiquitous/Darren Maybury pp.
**19** (top), **19** (bottom); © Eye Ubiquitous/Jonas Grau p. **21** (top); ©
Eye Ubiquitous/L. Fordyce p. **20** (left); © Getty Images/AFP PHOTO/
KARIM JAAFAR p. **9** (bottom); © Honda p. **4**; © Kawasaki Motors
Europe p. **5** (top); © MCN/EMAP p. **9** (top); © R. D. Battersby pp. **13**
(top), **24**, **25** (bottom); © Superstock/age fotostock p. **23** (top); ©
Suzuki PR Company p. **7** (bottom); © The Ronald Grant Archive pp.
**20** (right), **21** (bottom); © Travel Ink p. **16**; © Triumph Motorcycles
Ltd p. **12**.

Cover photograph reproduced with permission of © Getty Images/
AFP/Tengu Bahar. Background images by © istockphoto and ©
Corbis.

Every effort has been made to contact copyright holders of any
material reproduced in this book. Any omissions will be rectified in
subsequent printings if notice is given to the publishers.

**Disclaimer**
All the Internet addresses (URLs) given in this book were valid at
the time of going to press. However, due to the dynamic nature of
the Internet, some addresses may have changed, or sites may have
ceased to exist since publication. While the author and publishers
regret any inconvenience this may cause readers, no responsibility
for any such changes can be accepted by either the author or the
publishers.

# Ninja ▷

The Kawasaki Ninja ZX-14 has an engine that is bigger and more powerful than some car engines, but the bike is less than one third of a small car's weight. The combination of its 1,352 cc, 187-**horsepower** (**hp**) engine and such a light weight means the Ninja can reach a top speed of 300 kph (187 mph). This is almost as fast as a racing motorcycle. Like most sports motorcycles, it has a small windscreen at the front to deflect air over the rider's back.

# ▽ The purr-fect cat?

The Italian manufacturer, Ducati, is world-famous for producing motorcycles that are as beautiful to look at as they are fun to ride. One of their recent models, the 748, was described as "the perfect sports bike". For 2007, Ducati introduced a new and bigger top-of-the-range model, the 1098. It is the world's most powerful two-**cylinder** road-going motorcycle.

## DUCATI 1098

**Engine size**: 1099 cc

**Engine type**: L-twin

**Engine power**: 160 hp

**Top speed**: 290 kph (180 mph)

**Weight**: 173 kg

**Wheelbase**: 1,430 mm

# Sports roadsters

Sports "roadsters" are high-**performance** road motorcycles. They look similar to racing motorcycles and share many of the same design features.

The wheelbase (the distance between the front and rear wheels) is kept short. This makes the bike more agile and **manoeuvrable**. The weight of the bike is kept as low as possible to give it faster **acceleration** and a higher top speed. The rear wheel, which is driven by the engine, is wider than the front wheel. This is so that its tyre grips the road well. Only a small patch of rubber tyre is in contact with the ground at any one moment. This patch puts the whole of the motorcycle's engine power on the road.

## Smooth riding ▽

Sports motorcycle riders tuck themselves down behind the windscreen, like a jockey perched on a racehorse. It is not easy – riding with the weight on the hands can be quite tiring. They ride in this position because it offers the least resistance to air rushing past the bike. The motorcycle is also designed to cut **air resistance**. Its lumpy engine is surrounded by a **streamlined** cover, called a fairing, which deflects air smoothly around it. Cutting air resistance enables the bike to go faster.

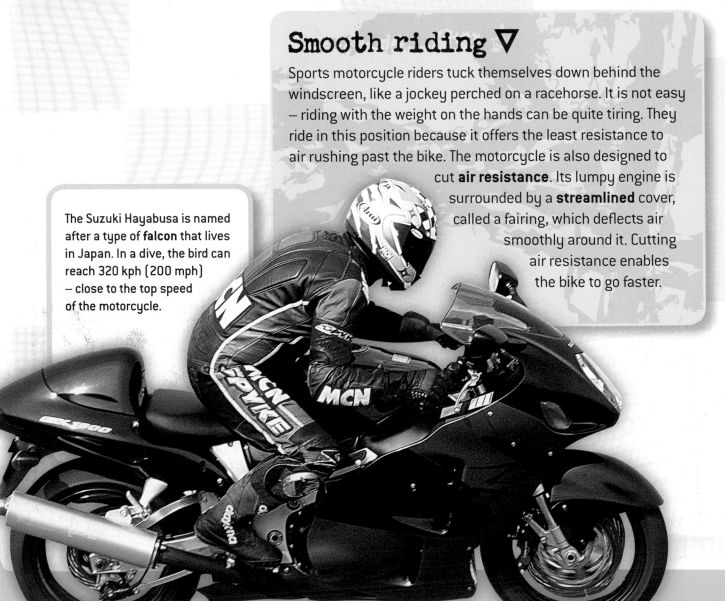

The Suzuki Hayabusa is named after a type of **falcon** that lives in Japan. In a dive, the bird can reach 320 kph (200 mph) – close to the top speed of the motorcycle.

# Braking ▷ distances

Sports motorcycles have disc brakes. They work by gripping a disc fixed to each wheel to slow it down. But the rider also has to read the road well. Higher speeds, as well as wet and loose surfaces, can more than double a motorcycle's **stopping distance**. Doubling a motorcycle's speed can quadruple the distance it takes to stop. A rider must also be careful not to brake too hard, as this could make the rear wheel skid.

dry road
– 50 kph
(31 mph)

Braking distance doubled

wet road
– 50 kph
(31 mph)

Speed doubled, braking distance quadrupled

dry road
– 100 kph
(62 mph)

## ▽ Slicing through the air

Designers of high-performance bikes like the Suzuki Hayabusa have to consider how air flows around the rider as well as the bike and its engine. They use computer **simulations** of air flowing around a **virtual** motorcycle and rider to try different shapes and find out which works best. Then real models are tested in a **wind tunnel** before the bike is built.

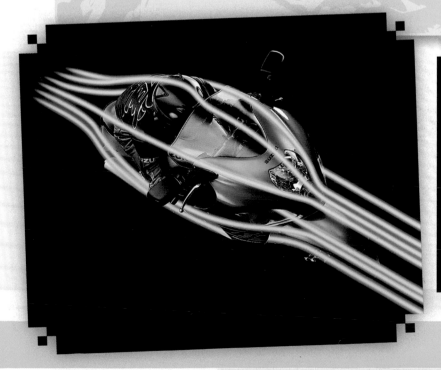

### SUZUKI GSX1300R HAYABUSA

**Engine size**: 1,299 cc

**Engine type**: 4-cylinder in-line

**Engine power**: 180 hp

**Top speed**: 305 kph (190 mph)

**Weight**: 217 kg

**Wheelbase**: 1,485 mm

# Racing machines

Many of the design features that make sports motorcycles so exciting to ride on the road were developed first for racing motorcycles. Racing motorcycles are divided into groups called classes. Each class has its own rules that cover things like engine size and the weight of the bike. They make sure that the bikes are closely matched in **performance** to make races more exciting. The challenge for designers is to create the best possible bike within the rules.

The **chassis** (frame) of a racing bike is especially important. It has to withstand the huge **acceleration**, braking, and cornering forces of racing without bending, twisting, or breaking. It also has to be as light as possible. It is very difficult to make parts that are both light and strong. However, it can be done by choosing lightweight materials such as **aluminium** or plastic. These are carefully designed into the right shape to give them extra strength.

## Grand Prix ▽

A motorcycle Grand Prix is one of a series of races that counts towards a world championship. All the motorcycles in each Grand Prix belong to the same class. There are three motorcycle Grand Prix classes: 125**cc**, 250cc, and MotoGP. The rules for each class change from year to year. In 2007, the biggest engine a MotoGP bike could have was reduced from 990cc to 800cc. The designers had to produce new bikes with the smaller engine.

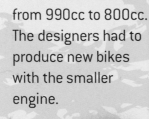

## ◁ Superbikes

One of the most popular racing classes is called Superbikes. Superbike racing motorcycles look similar to standard road motorcycles because strict rules limit how much the teams can modify them. As a result, success in Superbike racing often helps to sell more road motorcycles. The Italian motorcycle manufacturer Ducati has won more Superbike championships than all the other manufacturers added together.

Racing bikes line up on the starting grid for a Superbike race.

## MotoGP ▷

The MotoGP class began in 2002. About 20 riders compete in each race. During each racing season, about 18 races are held in 16 countries. The motorcycles that take part are technically very advanced. They are made of materials like **titanium**, a lightweight but very expensive metal, and carbon fibre. They also use advanced electronics to get the best performance from their engines.

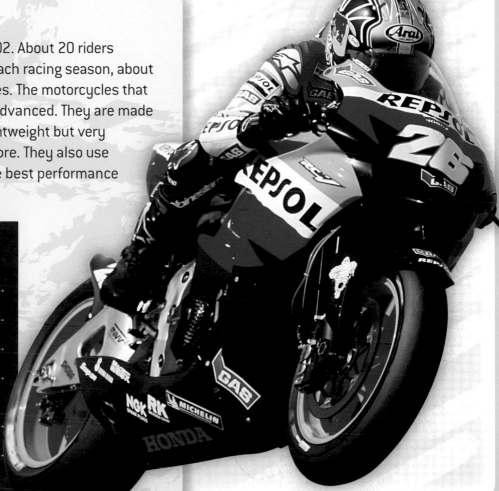

### HONDA RC212V 2007 MOTOGP RACER

**Engine size**: 800 cc

**Engine type**: V4

**Engine power**: 220+ hp

**Top speed**: 335+ kph (210+ mph)

**Weight**: 148 kg

**Wheelbase**: 1,440 mm

# Yamaha YZF-R1

## DESIGNER DREAMS

A successful motorcycle begins with a design brief – a set of goals. The Yamaha YZF-R1's designers were set three goals:

- to design the most powerful road-going sports motorcycle
- to make it lighter than its competitors
- to make it smaller than its competitors.

They started with a new four-**cylinder** engine. They laid it sideways across the motorcycle's width because this made the motorcycle shorter. Then they added a new **chassis**, the motorcycle's main frame. A motorcycle's chassis has to be strong enough to stop it twisting or bending. The Yamaha YZF-R1 is designed, like all modern motorcycles, so that the engine forms part of the chassis. The chassis reaches its full strength only when the engine is bolted to it!

## Lightweight lightning speed

Slimming down parts and choosing the right materials saves weight. Saving weight is important, because a lighter motorcycle **accelerates** faster. Choosing a new type of plastic meant that the Yamaha YZF-R1's designers could make its **bodywork** lighter. They chose **titanium** instead of steel for the exhaust **silencer**, because titanium is lighter. By saving a few grams here and there, kilograms were shaved off the motorcycle's total weight. Once the design was completed, **prototypes** were built to test it.

exhaust silencer

chassis

engine

fuel tank

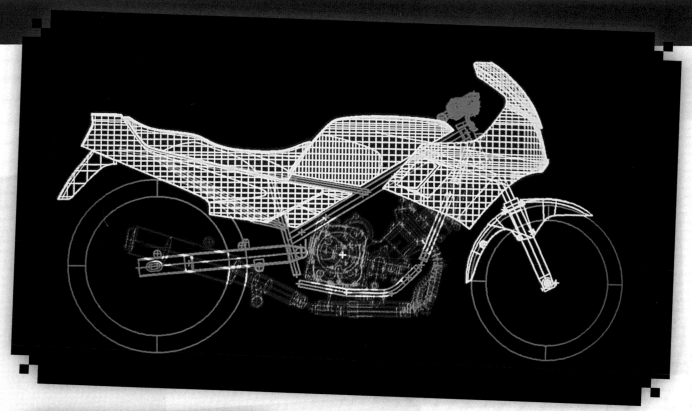

## CAD

Computer Aided Design (CAD) speeds up the design of complicated machines such as the Yamaha YZF-R1. It can show up problems at a very early stage. The designer can solve them before an expensive prototype is built

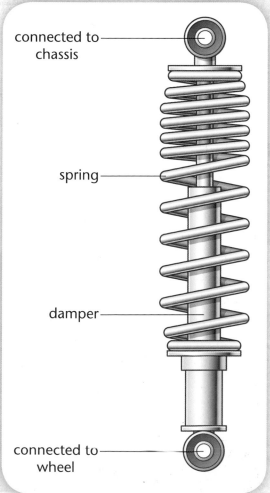

connected to chassis

spring

damper

connected to wheel

# Smoothing the ride

It is important to keep a motorcycle's wheels on the ground, because a wheel in the air cannot steer, brake, or transmit engine power to the road.

- Springs between the wheels and chassis give a smoother ride. They let the wheels follow bumps in the road without shaking the bike to bits.

- Each coiled spring works with a part called a damper. The damper's job is to stop the spring from bouncing too much and so to keep the wheel on the road.

CLOSER LOOK

CLOSER LOOK

CLOSER LOOK

# Yamaha YZF-R1
# A GRAND PRODUCTION

Once the design team has done its job and produced a new design, this has to be turned into a motorcycle that people can buy.

Taking a motorcycle from a design on a computer screen to a **production** model is complicated. There are a series of steps that have to be coordinated so that they come together in the right way at the right time. Standard "**off-the-shelf**" parts have to be ordered in the right numbers. Parts designed specially for the new motorcycle have to be made. A production line, where the motorcycle will be built, has to be set up. All the parts have to be delivered to the production line at the right time so that there are no hold-ups. Meanwhile, the new model is shown to the public and press, so that everyone knows about it. Finally, thousands of the new motorcycles are sent out to dealers all over the world.

## Production line

Motorcycles are built on a factory production line, like this one at a Triumph factory. Parts made in other factories are delivered to the production line and bolted together. In many factories, parts are moved around automatically to ensure that they are in the right place when needed. As each bike moves along the line, workers add more and more parts until a finished motorcycle is wheeled off the end. Every motorcycle is then checked and tested.

## From shipping to showroom

Newly-built motorcycles are packed in crates and loaded onto ships. The crates are specially designed to protect the bikes during their long journeys. The ships sail to ports all over the world. On arrival, they are unloaded and transported by truck to motorcycle dealers. There, they are uncrated and put on display in a showroom where customers can finally get a closer look at them.

## Getting the message out

Marketing is an essential part of selling a motorcycle. Its aim is to tell people about its design, so that they will want to buy it. This involves telling people what the motorcycle looks like, what its new design features are, and how well it performs.

- Advertisements placed in magazines are designed to give the motorcycle an attractive image.
- Brochures are sent to motorcycle dealers to give to their customers.
- The motorcycle itself also appears at motorcycle shows where people can see it.
- A few motorcycles are loaned to motorcycling journalists, so that they can write magazine articles about them.

CLOSER LOOK

## CLOSER LOOK

# Yamaha YZF-R1
# DESIGNED TO PLEASE

Designers do not just design the parts of a motorcycle. They also design its **performance**. The Yamaha YZF-R1's performance has been carefully designed to please its riders.

The YZF-R1 has to give a thrilling ride, but it also has to be safe for the riders. Although it looks similar to a racing motorcycle, its designers have deliberately made it **handle** differently from a racing motorcycle. It accelerates quickly enough to be exciting, but not so quickly that it needs a professional rider to control it. Its **suspension** system is made soft enough to soak up bumps in the road, but hard enough to stop the bike diving at the front when the rider brakes hard. A racing motorcycle's suspension is much harder, which can make it uncomfortable to ride and difficult to control, especially on rough ground.

## Riding position

A sports motorcycle rider leans forward over the motorcycle's **fuel** tank. The shape of the YZF-R1 helps keep the rider in the right position. When the bike accelerates hard, the rider is forced backwards. The motorcycle's raised seat-back stops the rider sliding back. When the bike brakes hard, the rider is thrown forwards. However, there are cut-outs in the fuel tank for the rider to grip with his or her knees to stop this.

raised seat-back

fuel tank cut-out

# Wheels

A motorcycle's spinning wheels act like gyroscopes. A gyroscope is a spinning wheel that stays in the same position even if someone tries to turn it or push it over. The gyroscope effect helps to keep a motorcycle upright. However, the same effect also makes it more difficult to lean the bike over and make it turn. That is why you often see racing motorcyclists hanging off the side of their motorcycles, pulling them over to take a corner. Yamaha made the YZF-R1's wheels lighter to reduce this gyroscope effect and make the bike easier to steer.

Designers have to be careful not to make a motorcycle either too easy or too difficult to ride, or it won't have precisely the right sports performance its riders want.

## YAMAHA YZF-R1

**Engine size**: 998 cc

**Engine type**: 4-cylinder in line

**Engine power**: 180 hp

**Top speed**: 295 kph (184 mph)

**Weight**: 177 kg

**Wheelbase**: 1,415 mm

CLOSER LOOK

# Engine power

Sports motorcycles need powerful engines for their agile **performance**. The bigger and more powerful an engine is, the heavier it is, but sports motorcycles need to be light. Engine designers are constantly looking for ways of cutting the weight of an engine without reducing its power. Using lightweight **aluminium** instead of steel is one answer. Motorcycle engines work like car engines. **Fuel** and air are sucked into a **cylinder** inside the engine. A **spark plug** creates a spark that explodes the mixture. The hot gases expand and push a **piston** down the cylinder. The up-and-down movement of the pistons in the cylinders drives the motorcycle's rear wheel. Most motorcycles have between one and four cylinders.

## Twin ▷ power

The Harley-Davidson Springer Softail is powered by a popular motorcycle engine called a V-twin. It has two cylinders set at an angle to each other, forming a V-shape. The low rumbling sound of a big Harley V-twin is unmistakable.

# Cooling off

Burning fuel inside an engine heats up the whole engine. To stop it heating up too much, it is cooled by using air or water.

- Most motorcycle engines are air-cooled. The cylinders are fitted with metal **fins** to give them a huge **surface area**. Air blowing around the fins absorbs some of their heat and carries it away.

- The biggest motorcycle engines are water-cooled. Water circulates through the engine and carries heat away to a **radiator**. Air blowing through the radiator cools the water, which goes back to the engine.

# Boxing clever ▷

The BMW R1200 GS has a type of engine called a boxer. Most motorcycle engines have cylinders that stand up on end, next to each other. A boxer's cylinders lie flat, end-to-end across the width of the motorcycle. They are called horizontally opposed cylinders. A two-cylinder boxer is also called a flat twin. The wide shape of a boxer means that its cylinders stick out into the air rushing past the bike, keeping them cool.

## ◁ Superpower

The Dodge Tomahawk is a monster of a motorcycle. It is powered by a massive 500 **horsepower** engine that usually powers a Dodge Viper supercar. The huge engine gives the bike an astonishing top speed of at least 480 kph (300 mph). Only ten of these bikes will be sold. Each one will cost about half a million US dollars!

| BMW R1200 GS | |
|---|---|
| **Engine size**: 1,170 cc | |
| **Engine type**: flat twin | |
| **Engine power**: 100 hp | |
| **Top speed**: 200+ kph (125+ mph) | |
| **Weight**: 199 kg | |
| **Wheelbase**: 1,507 mm | |

cylinder

# ▷ Drag-bikes

The fastest two-wheeled sport on a track is drag-bike racing. Drag motorcycles are designed to do one thing — **accelerate** as fast as they can in a straight line.

Drag-bikes do not have to turn any corners or overtake other motorcycles. They race two at a time down a straight track a quarter-of-a-mile (402 metres) long. Like racing cars, drag-bikes are divided into a series of classes. The fastest drag-bikes belong to the Top **Fuel** class, which lets designers do almost anything in the search for speed. The challenge for the designer is to produce a machine that turns engine power into acceleration as fast as possible.

## Getting tyred ▽

A drag-bike's back tyre is big and wide because it has to transmit an enormous amount of engine power onto the track. Putting more rubber on the track gives better grip. Better grip means faster acceleration. The front tyre is smaller and thinner. Its job is to keep the motorcycle running straight.

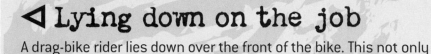

## ◁ Lying down on the job

A drag-bike rider lies down over the front of the bike. This not only cuts down **air resistance**, it also helps to weigh down the front of the bike. The engine is so powerful that it can lift the front wheel off the ground as the bike roars away from the start line. Some bikes need the extra help of a long frame, called a wheelie bar, at the back to stop the front from rearing up.

## Burning out ▽

Soft rubber grips a track better than hard rubber, and rubber is softer when it warms up. So, a drag-bike's big rear tyre is warmed up just before a race. It is done by a spectacular activity called burning-out. With the front brake firmly applied so the bike does not move, the rider revs the engine so that the rear wheel spins and slips on the ground. **Friction** between the tyre and the ground heats the tyre so much that clouds of thick smoke pour off it.

### LARRY MCBRIDE TOP FUEL DRAG-BIKE

**Engine size**: 1,400 cc

**Engine type**: 4-cylinder

**Engine power**: 1,000 hp

**Top speed**: 390 kph (245 mph)

**Weight**: 467 kg

**Wheelbase**: 2,540 mm

A drag-bike's rear tyre does not last long. It may have to be replaced after only eight races. A Top Fuel race can be over within five seconds, so a rear tyre's lifetime may be less than one minute!

# Modern classics

New motorcycles appear nearly every month. They have the latest technology and materials, but not always the latest style or shape. Some riders prefer the classic styling of motorcycles from years ago. For these people, manufacturers make new motorcycles that look similar to those that were made up to 60 years ago. Making new motorcycles that look like old models is called **retro**-styling. Many of these motorcycles were made famous by Hollywood movies about young Americans growing up in the 1950s. The popularity of the films increased demand for the motorcycles ridden by their stars.

Harley-Davidson is one of the most successful manufacturers of retro-styled motorcycles. When British and then Japanese motorcycles flooded into America in the 1950s and 1960s, Harley-Davidson concentrated on making motorcycles with traditional styling. Their unique looks made them stand out from the rest. They proved to be very successful, and they still are. Other manufacturers are now producing retro-styled motorcycles, too.

## Movie magic ▷

Marlon Brando (right) looked cool and dangerous on his 650**cc** Triumph Thunderbird in the 1954 movie *The Wild One*. Images like this, and of police officers patrolling US highways on their Harley-Davidsons, created a demand for these motorcycles that has lasted to the present day.

## ◁ King of the road

The Harley-Davidson Road King looks as if it came straight out of the 1950s. Although it looks like an old motorcycle, it is actually a modern motorcycle designed and built using the most modern methods and materials. Harley-Davidson produces more than a dozen motorcycles that have classic styling taken from the 1940s and 1950s.

## Custom design ▽

Bikers often try to make their motorcycles look a little different from everyone else's by adding different accessories. It is called personalizing or customizing. The height of the custom motorcycle craze was in the 1950s and 1960s, when the chopper motorcycle appeared. It was a motorcycle that was stripped down to its essential parts. Some choppers had long front **forks** and tall handlebars called "ape-hangers". Many of these extraordinary chopper motorcycles were based on Harley-Davidson models.

### HARLEY-DAVIDSON FLHR ROAD KING

**Engine size**: 1,584 cc

**Engine type**: V-twin

**Engine power**: 68 hp

**Top speed**: 185 kph (115 mph)

**Weight**: 332 kg

**Wheelbase**: 1,610 mm

# Accidents

No matter how well designed vehicles are, road accidents will carry on happening because drivers and riders make mistakes. Riding a motorcycle is a fine balance between power and gravity. And things can go wrong.

A motorcycle on the road or the racetrack is normally under control only when both wheels grip the ground. A skid or a slide is bad news. Cornering too fast can make a motorcycle slide across the road. Turning on the power too quickly can make a wheel spin. Braking too hard can start a skid. Something mechanical can fail or go wrong on the motorcycle. Even if the rider does not make a mistake and the motorcycle works perfectly, other road users can cause accidents. Moving vehicles have a lot of energy. The faster a vehicle goes, the more energy it has and the more damage it can do if it comes to a sudden stop in an accident. That is why it is important to stick to speed limits on public roads.

## Sliding out ▽

A motorcyclist leans over in a bend to balance the cornering force that tries to topple the motorcycle over. You can feel this sideways force when you go round a corner in a car. When a motorcycle leans over, it rides on the side of its tyres. If the road is wet or oily, or the rider corners too fast, the tyres lose grip. The motorcycle slides towards the outside of the bend.

## Difficult to see ▷

Accidents involving motorcycles often happen because a motorcycle is so much smaller and narrower than many other vehicles. A car driver overtaking other traffic or turning can fail to see a motorcycle, with disastrous results. Wearing bright clothing can help to make the motorcycle rider more easily seen. Many motorcycles have lights that come on automatically when the engine is started, so the motorcycle is more visible.

## ◁ Keeping it balanced

A motorcycle needs to be kept upright and balanced. The motorcycle's design helps the rider to do this. The heaviest part of a motorcycle is its engine. Keeping this as low as possible makes the motorcycle more stable and less likely to topple over. Imagine how much harder it would be to walk with heavy shopping bags above your head instead of held down low.

While most drivers are protected inside their vehicles by seatbelts, **airbags**, and soft surfaces, a motorcycle rider has no protection. It is vital that motorcyclists wear clothes designed to protect them if the worst should happen.

The most delicate and vulnerable part of a motorcyclist's body is the brain. So, the most important piece of motorcycle safety clothing is a helmet. It protects the head in three ways. The hard outer shell saves the head from injuries caused by an impact with a solid object. Then the soft lining inside the helmet cushions the head. Finally, a shatter-proof visor shields the rider's eyes.

## Skid lids ▷

The most popular type of motorcycle helmet is the full-face type (left). It covers the whole head and face, and it has a clear visor on the front for the rider to look through. Some of these helmets have a flip-up front, so that the rider can talk to people without having to take the helmet off. Police motorcyclists sometimes wear this type. Riders of classic or **retro**-styled bikes often wear an older style of open-face helmet, called a "jet helmet" (right) because it looks like a helmet worn by a fighter pilot.

SUPERBIKES

## Wearing leather △

A racing motorcyclist wears a leather suit for two reasons. As well as giving protection from scrapes and burns, it also gives the rider a **streamlined** shape. This helps the air to slide smoothly over the rider's back. Cutting **air resistance** makes the motorcycle faster. This is important because races are often so close that saving a fraction of a second on each lap of a circuit can make the difference between winning and losing.

## Backing up ▽

After the head, the most vulnerable part of a rider's body is the spine. It carries the **nerves** that control the arms and legs, so a damaged spine can result in a rider having to use a wheelchair to get around. Racing motorcyclists and some road riders wear a hard pad, called a back protector or spine board, over their spine. Some leathers have a built-in back protector.

## Suit yourself

The rest of the rider's body is protected by a tough jacket and trousers. They save the rider's skin from being scraped along the ground. Racing motorcyclists and some road motorcycle riders wear a one-piece leather suit. Leather gloves and boots complete the outfit. Even with the best equipment, motorcycling can be dangerous, so riders have to be careful.

# Record setters

The motorcycles that set speed records look more like guided missiles than motorcycles. Their extraordinary shape helps them to go as fast as a small jet-aeroplane! The faster a vehicle is designed to go, the more important its shape becomes. The right shape creates the least **air resistance** and lets the motorcycle go faster.

Long, slender motorcycles, called streamliners, set the fastest speed records. They pierce the air like an arrow. To squeeze as much engine power as possible into the slim body, they often have two engines, one in front of the other. Riders normally sit on top of a motorcycle, but land-speed-record challengers are sealed inside their motorcycle so that they do not spoil the smooth flow of air over its body.

To attempt a new land-speed record, a motorcycle must go as fast as possible between two markers, then turn round and come back again. The time for the bike to go between the markers is measured very accurately and this time is used to calculate the bike's speed. Then the average speed for the two runs is calculated.

## Bonneville ▷ Salt Flats

A long, flat patch of ground is essential for setting land-speed records. Motorcycle records have been set at the Bonneville Salt Flats in Utah, USA, since the 1950s. The area is baked by the summer sun, forming a hard, flat surface of 260 square kilometres (100 square miles). The black line in the photo is a guide for riders attempting to break records.

# Easyriders ▷

In 1990, Dave Campos (right) set a motorcycle land-speed record of 518 kph (322 mph) in his streamliner, called Easyriders. His record stood for 16 years until September 4, 2006, when Rocky Robinson rode his Ack Attack streamliner to a speed of 551 kph (342 mph). This record stood for only one day!

# BUB 7 ▽

On September 5, 2006, Chris Carr was sealed inside the BUB 7 streamliner and set off across the Bonneville Salt Flats. He made his first run at 569 kph (354 mph). Then he turned around and made his return run at 558 kph (347 mph). The official timekeepers worked out his average speed over the two runs as 563 kph (350 mph), a new record.

## BUB 7 LAND SPEED RECORD HOLDER

**Engine size**: 2,995 cc

**Engine type**: V4

**Engine power**: 500 hp

**Top speed**: 570 kph (355 mph)

**Weight**: 770 Kg

**Wheelbase**: 4,880 mm

# ▷ Data files

As we have seen, there are many different types of sports motorcycle. Each has been designed with a particular type of rider in mind. This table of information compares the basic specifications (details) and **performance** of some of today's best-known sports motorcycles.

| Motorcycle | Engine size (cc) | Engine power (horsepower) | Top speed (kph / mph) | Number of cylinders | Weight (kilograms) | Wheelbase (millimetres) |
|---|---|---|---|---|---|---|
| BMW R1200 GS | 1,170 | 100 | 200 / 125 | 2 | 199 | 1,507 |
| BUB 7 record holder | 2,995 | 500 | 570 / 355 | 4 | 770 | 4,880 |
| Ducati 1098 | 1,099 | 160 | 290 / 180 | 2 | 173 | 1,430 |
| Harley-Davidson FLHR Road King | 1,584 | 68 | 185 / 115 | 2 | 332 | 1,610 |
| Honda CBR1000RR Fireblade | 998 | 172 | 275 / 170 | 4 | 176 | 1,402 |
| Honda RC212V MotoGP racer | 800 | 220 | 335 / 210 | 4 | 148 | 1,440 |
| Kawasaki Ninja ZX-14 | 1,352 | 187 | 300 / 187 | 4 | 218 | 1,460 |
| Larry McBride Top Fuel drag bike | 1,400 | 1,000 | 390 / 245 | 4 | 467 | 2,540 |
| Suzuki GSX1300R Hayabusa | 1,299 | 180 | 305 / 190 | 4 | 217 | 1,485 |
| Vyrus 985C3 4V | 999 | 150 | 290 / 180 | 2 | 157 | 1,375 |
| Yamaha YZF-R1 | 998 | 180 | 295 / 184 | 4 | 177 | 1,415 |

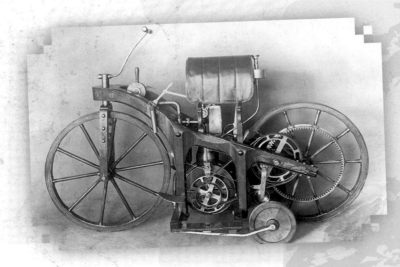

## ◁ The first motorcycle

The very first motorcycle was not exactly a superbike! It was a heavy wooden vehicle with a **265cc** engine built by the German engineer Gottlieb Daimler in 1885. It had a top speed of about 12 kph (7.5 mph)! It needed two small stabilizer wheels to help keep it upright. There had been steam-powered bicycles as far back as 1869, but the Daimler motorcycle was the first to have a petrol engine.

## Books

*Motorcycles*, Chris Oxlade (Heinemann Library, 2007)
*Ultimate Motorbikes*, Roland Brown (J. H. Haynes, 2006)
*Motorbikes*, David Jefferis (Raintree, 2004)
*Mega Book of Motorcycles*, Lynne Gibbs (Belitha Press, 2002)

## Websites

http://news.bbc.co.uk/sport1/hi/motorsport/motorbikes/default.htm
The part of the vast BBC website that deals with motorcycle sport.

http://auto.howstuffworks.com/motorcycle.htm
All about how motorcycles work.

http://www.nationalmotorcyclemuseum.co.uk
The world's biggest motorcycle museum, in Britain.

## Racing ▷

Motorcycle racing began in France in 1894. It quickly spread to other countries. The desire to win races encouraged motorcycle manufacturers and racing teams to produce faster motorcycles. Many of the advances made in the need for speed were later built into road motorcycles. The first races were held on ordinary roads, but soon racetracks were being built for both car and motorcycle races. The world's first purpose-built racetrack was opened at Brooklands, in England, in 1907. The photograph on the right is of a motorcycle race at Brooklands in the mid-1920s.

# Glossary

**accelerate** go faster. A motorcycle rider accelerates by twisting the handgrip at the end of the right handlebar. That sends more fuel into the engine, which speeds up and turns the motorcycle's rear wheel faster.

**airbag** a safety device fitted to some cars. If the car crashes, an airbag in the steering wheel inflates in a fraction of a second and cushions the driver's head. Some cars have several different airbags in different places to protect passengers too.

**air resistance** the slowing effect of air on any object, including a motorcycle, that tries to move through air. Making a motorcycle more smooth and streamlined reduces air resistance, allowing it to go faster.

**aluminium** a lightweight metal that is easy to bend and shape. It is often used to make parts of motorcycles lighter than they would be if made from steel.

**bodywork** the smooth outer shell of a motorcycle

**cc** cubic centimetre. In motorcycling, the cc figure refers to the size (capacity) of the engine's cylinders, where the fuel is burned. In the USA this is measured in cubic inches. An 88 cubic inch Harley-Davidson engine is equivalent to 1,449cc.

**chassis** a motorcycle's main frame – the rest of the motorcycle is bolted onto it

**cylinder** the tube-shaped part of an engine, where the fuel is burned

**falcon** a bird of prey

**fins** thin pieces of metal attached to part of an engine to help cool it down. Air blowing around the fins absorbs some of their heat.

**fork** part of a motorcycle's suspension system. A spring and damper inside a metal tube sit on each side of the front wheel, like two prongs of a fork.

**friction** a force that tries to slow down moving objects when they slide over each other

**fuel** the substance that is burned inside a motorcycle engine. This releases energy, which is converted into movement. Most motorcycles burn ordinary petrol. Some drag-bikes burn special fuels designed to release energy even faster than normal petrol.

**handling** how a motorcycle responds when it is being driven, and how well it holds the road while moving

**horsepower (hp)** a unit of engine power equal to the rate of work of one horse. This is calculated to be 746 watts.

**manoeuvrable** able to be steered nimbly and sharply

**nerves** fibres that carry electrical impulses between the brain and other parts of the body. Information from the senses travels to the brain along nerves, and electric signals sent out by the brain to control the muscles also travel along nerves.

**off-the-shelf** ready-made. Off-the-shelf parts are existing parts that can be bought in from a supplier and do not have to be specially designed and made.

**performance** the way a vehicle functions – its speed, acceleration, and stability

**piston** the part of a motorcycle engine that slides up and down inside a cylinder. Burning fuel inside the cylinder pushes the piston down and drives the motorcycle's rear wheel.

**production motorcycles** motorcycles that are produced in large numbers for sale to the general public

**prototype** the first model of a new vehicle, built for testing

**radiator** part of an engine's cooling system. Water heated by the engine flows through thin pipes in the radiator. Air blowing around the pipes cools the water, which returns to the engine.

**retro** back or backwards. A retro-style motorcycle is a modern motorcycle that looks like a motorcycle from the past.

**silencer** the part of a motorcycle's engine that reduces engine noise. The silencer is fitted to the engine's exhaust pipe or pipes. These carry waste gases out of the engine after the fuel has been burned.

**simulation** a copy of an object, problem, or situation created inside a computer. A whole motorcycle can be created, or simulated, in a computer. It can then be tested to see how the real motorcycle will behave in different conditions and at different speeds.

**spark plug** the part of a motorcycle's engine that makes an electrical spark to burn the fuel in the cylinder. Each cylinder inside the engine has its own spark plug.

**stopping distance** the distance a motorcycle travels from when the rider applies the brakes until it comes to a halt

**streamlined** an object shaped so that air flows smoothly around it. Streamlining is more important the faster a motorcycle goes. Slower cruisers and tourers do not need to be very streamlined. Faster racing and sports bikes have a streamlined covering called a fairing to make air flow smoothly around them.

**surface area** the size of the outside face of something. The fins on an air-cooled motorcycle engine are there to give it a bigger surface area, to give up more heat to the surrounding air.

**suspension** the set of springs and other devices that connect a motorcycle's frame to its axles. The suspension system lets the wheels follow bumps and hollows in the ground, while the rest of the motorcycle moves along more smoothly.

**titanium** very strong, yet lightweight, metal that is used for making some parts of a motorcycle. Titanium is more expensive than steel and more difficult to make parts from, so it is used only where its light weight or resistance to high temperatures is needed.

**virtual** not real. The plan, or design, of a motorcycle that appears on a computer screen is not real. It exists in the computer's memory and on the screen. It is a virtual motorcycle.

**wind tunnel** a large tube or passage that air is blown through. Models of motorcycles and full-size motorcycles are tested by placing them in a wind tunnel and studying how air flows around them.

# Index